dose : plays & monologues

BOOKS BY DAN BERNITT
AVAILABLE FROM SAWYER HOUSE

Dose: Plays & Monologues

INCLUDES:
Almost
Thanks for the Scabies, Jerkface!
Button-Down Showgirl
My Parents Talk to Stuffed Animals

Phi Alpha Gamma

dose : plays & monologues

☙

dan bernitt

SAWYER HOUSE
LEXINGTON
2008

SAWYER HOUSE
PO BOX 1415, LEXINGTON, KY 40588-1415

Copyright © 2006, 2007, 2008 by Dan Bernitt
All rights reserved
Printed in the United States of America

FIRST EDITION, November 2007;
SECOND EDITION, November 2008.

Publisher's Cataloging-in-Publication Data
Bernitt, Dan (1986–).
    Dose: plays and monologues / by Dan Bernitt. —2ND ed.
    p. cm.
    ISBN-13: 978-0-9821560-1-8
    ISBN-10: 0-9821560-1-4
    I. Title.

Library of Congress Control Number: 2008908934

Cover photograph by Ben Earwicker
    (www.garrisonphoto.org)
Author photograph © 2006 by Vidyuta Rangnekar
    (www.fivebyfivegallery.com)

www.sawyerhouse.net

CAUTION: Professionals and amateurs are hereby warned that the contents of *Dose: Plays & Monologues* are subject to a royalty. The contents are fully protected under the copyright laws of the United States and all countries covered by the International Copyright Union (including the Dominion of Canada and the rest of the British Commonwealth) and of all countries covered by the Pan-American Copyright Convention and the Universal Copyright Convention, and of all countries with which the United States has reciprocal copyright relations. All rights, including professional, amateur, motion picture, recitation, lecturing, public reading, radio broadcasting, television, video or sound taping, all other forms of mechanical or electronic reproduction, such as information storage and retrieval systems and photocopying, and the rights of translation into foreign languages, are strictly reserved. Particular emphasis is laid upon the question of readings, permission for which must be secured from the author in writing.

for trish and tonya

contents.

Almost	1
Thanks for the Scabies, Jerkface!	67
Button-Down Showgirl	141
My Parents Talk to Stuffed Animals	159

Almost

Thanks for the Scabies, Jerkface!

Button-Down Showgirl

My Parents Talk to Stuffed Animals

"... the discourse of masculinity can be very funny in a tragic sort of way. Male heterosexuality can be understood as a tragicomic experience. Frequently, though, the actors apprehend neither the humor nor the misery."

PETER F. MURPHY,
Studs, Tools, and the Family Jewels

acknowledgements.

The author would like to thank
Herman Daniel Farrell III and Carolyn Sesbeau.

characters.
(in order of appearance)

PAUL, early twenties
MARK, early twenties
BARTENDER*, late twenties or early thirties
AMY, early twenties
ADAM, nineteen
FATHER*, early-to-mid fifties
RON, seventeen
JAKE, sixteen
MOM, early-to-mid forties

Asterisk indicates non-speaking role.

I.

Scene: Now. An American pub, but with another break-in it'd be a dive. The wooden floors have seen significantly cleaner days. When opened, the front wooden door brings in the occasional touch of an autumn draft. The main room's bar is lined with bar stools: some of the leather upholstering is cracked, all are worn and, only in this light, the same color. Along the exposed brick walls are built-in tables; bar stools rest underneath. PAUL *and* MARK *sit at one of these tables; they aren't yet regulars to this fine establishment, but another few visits might promote them. Their table is next to a large glass window. A couple PBRs rest empty on their table. The muted sound of a downtown street: chatter, commotion, the occasional siren.*

PAUL

'Nother beer? It's last call.

MARK

Yeah, dude. Sure.

PAUL

Same kind?

MARK

Yeah, sure.

(PAUL gets two beers, pays the bartender.)

PAUL

Another PBR: pretty bad and wretched.
   (Raising his bottle.)
Cheers. To Saturday night.

MARK

Thanks. Cheers.
   (They tap bottles.)
And, that'd be PBW, dumbass.
   (Chuckles.)
You've been thinkin' of that all night, haven't you?

PAUL

Naw, I thought, y'know. Wretched, like "retch," like puke. Like, PBR makes me want to puke. Well, yeah, retch starts with an R, so I thought — it's not even worth explaining. Screw you, man.

MARK

You wish you could.
   (Pause.)
Aw, c'mon, it was a joke, bro.
   (Pause.)
Paul – dude –

PAUL

I'm just messin' with ya.

MARK

Damn it, Paul. I can never tell if you're fuckin' with me. Asshole.

PAUL

Heh. Yeah, I get it from my brother.

MARK

Really? Your asshole?

PAUL

Ha. No, Adam and I, we'd always get in fights when we were in high school. Like, fistfights.

MARK

Over what?

PAUL

Oh, nothing.
 (Pause.)
Y– y'know– we– we were just messin' around with each other. We'd wrestle and stuff. Whenever I'd pin him or whenever I'd punch him hard, he'd act hurt. Like, silent doubled-over kinda hurt. Y'know, I thought I'd like really hurt him or something. So's, I'd ask if he was alright. And, then, the guy'd knock me over, throw me to the ground. S'like, he'd knock me down cold, man. Then, while, like, I'm tryin' to get free, he'd always shout at me, like, "Never let your guard down, never let your guard down."
 (Short laugh.)
That jerk.

MARK

So you do it to me now?

PAUL

(With a laugh.)
Yeah. Y'know, and everyone else.

MARK

Jerk.

PAUL

But I gotcha! What, you never had anything like that when you were younger?

MARK

Nope, we were pretty straight-laced. Dad didn't horse around much. Well, my brother, we'd horse around a bit. Mom always wanted us to stop; afraid we'd break somethin'.

PAUL

Hah. What's your bro like?

MARK

Jake? He was pretty great.

PAUL

Yeah, cool, man.
  (Pause.)
Wait – wait, "was?" He's not great anymore?

MARK

Actually, J– Jake passed away a few years ago.

He and my mom, they both...

PAUL

Oh.
(Laughs.)
Oh, I get it.

MARK

Yeah, heehaw, Paul. My mom and brother are dead.

PAUL

Naw, man. Ya can't joke about death like that. Man, it's, like, in the rules of faking people out. Ya can't just talk about death like that.

MARK

I'm not.

PAUL

Aw, c'mon, man. Your folks aren't dead. I saw your mom last year, she was helpin' you move into the dorms.
(Pause.)
A-ha! I gotcha. Man, you can't beat this; I totally saw your mom in the dorm.
(Pause.)
Why aren't y—

MARK

Remarried?

PAUL

Mark. C'mon.
(Pause.)
Oh, wow, man. You aren't joking. Man, I'm so sorry.

MARK

S'alright.

PAUL

It's just, y'know...

MARK

Paul, don't worry about it, dude. You didn't know.

PAUL

It was a jerk thing to do.

MARK

Well, yeah, you pretty much are.
(Pause.)
No, I don't mean that. You aren't a jerk. Just did a jerk thing. But, hey. Dude. I'm fine talkin' about it. If you are, too.

PAUL

(Nodding, careful with words.)
Yeah. How'd they pass?

MARK

Was a car accident. I was 17. Jake was 16, didn't have his license yet. So Mom drove him and his girlfriend on a date They dropped her off at her house and were on their way home. Someone hit 'em. Hit and run, dude. Both wearin' their seatbelts, too.

PAUL

When was this?

MARK

Whew, um. Fall? Yeah, early November. Four years ago. Sure made Thanksgiving and Christmas a ball.

PAUL

I'm sorry, man. Wait – and your dad remarried that soon?

MARK

I don't wanna talk about that part.

PAUL

That's fine, man.

MARK

Just nothing you ever expect. Burying your mom and little brother.

PAUL

Yeah.

MARK

I dunno, dude. I hate to say something as sick as this, but, y'know, it's easier to lose your parents. Well, compared to burying your little brother.

I mean, you expect to outlive your parents, right? But to see him lying there. Goddamn. I mean, he was a guy about your size. Dark hair, too.
(Pause.)
Eyes just shut. Shut.

PAUL

They're in good hands, though.

MARK

Yeah, I like to believe stuff like that. Makes coping kinda easier. Still hard though. Only so much you can take.

PAUL

No more than you can bare. Trust me, man.

MARK

Thanks.
(He takes a swig of beer.)
How's Amy?

PAUL

Sh-she's well. A year last month.

MARK

Congrats, dude.

PAUL

Yeah, thanks.

MARK

She the one?

PAUL

Might.
(Pause.)
Yeah, probably.

MARK

That's cool, man. You're lucky.

PAUL

You not dating?

MARK

Hah. Nope. Can't seem to keep a relationship going.

PAUL

Yeah. It's hard. But you'll know when you've found it.
(The BARTENDER has packed up during their conversation and stands waiting.)
Oh, looks like he's kickin' us out now.
(Quietly joking, to MARK)
Shuttin' down our place, man.

MARK

Yeah. Can't compete with bar time, I guess.

PAUL

Yeah. I should head back to Amy's now anyway. She's probably waitin'.

MARK

Oh, shit, dude. I didn't know you had to be

anywhere.

PAUL

Nah, man. It was good seeing you.

MARK

Yeah. You too, bro.

(Together, MARK and PAUL walk out of the bar. The door slams shut, and the bartender begins closing: dimming lights, locking the door. Standing on the sidewalk under the sterile intensity of the streetlight, the sound of the street envelopes MARK and PAUL; while they can still be heard, there is more effort in their interaction.)

PAUL

You goin' this way?

MARK

Nah, over there.

PAUL

How you gettin' home?

MARK

Oh, it's not too far. I'll walk.

PAUL

I have my car, man. I could stop by your place on my way to Amy's.

MARK
You're driving?

PAUL
Yeah, I'm fine, man. Just a little buzz.

MARK
Sure?

PAUL
Absolutely. No worries, man.

MARK
Alright. Take it easy. Shit, it's almost three.

PAUL
Yeah. It is.

MARK
Will I see you later?

PAUL
Um, yeah, I hope. Sometime, man. Gimme a call this weekend.

MARK
Cool. Night, dude.

PAUL
(Extending a handshake.)
Peace.

MARK
(Laughs.)
Fuck that, gimme a hug.

PAUL
(Blocking MARK.)
Dude. What?

MARK
A. Hug. A hug?

PAUL
No.
(Pause.)
Hah, man. I'm buzzed, but I'm not drunk.

MARK
(Moving in.)
Dude, it's a hug.

PAUL
Man, stop.

MARK
What, afraid I'm gonna grab yer ass?

PAUL
Don't touch me.

MARK
Dude —

PAUL

Don't!

MARK

Alright. I. Won't give you a hug goodb–

PAUL

I'm not like that.

MARK

Neither am I. Peace. Drive safe, bro.

(MARK exits, leaving PAUL alone. A long pause.)

II.

Scene: in memory. Chronologically, all memory scenes take place prior to the bar scene and as indicated by the stage directions. A sense of place should be established using minimal props or set pieces. Visually, these scenes can take in place in front of the dimly lit bar, illuminating both past and present.

Earlier that night. MARK *sits alone in his one-bedroom apartment. The brief, jarring sound of sirens. He flips open his cell phone and begins searching through numbers to call. He dials one.*

MARK

Hey, Molly. Hey, it's Mark. Yeah, how've you been? Right. Yeah, cool. Hey, do you wanna get coffee sometime tonight? You're out with your boyfriend. Okay. Yeah, that's cool. Yeah, next week sounds good. Oh, shi— oh, no, no, Thursday's no good for me. Yeah. Well, I'll see you in class, we can work it out then. Okay, sounds good. You too. Bye, Mol.
    (He sighs. Mouths "boyfriend." Chuckles to himself. Dials another number.)
Sco-o-ott. Hey, it's Mark. Yeah, buddy, I'm doing

well. Yourself? (*Hearty laughter.*) You're kidding. (*Laughs.*) You're kidding me. (*Chuckles.*) That's crazy. Hey, you wanna get a beer tonight? Aw, yeah, that's right. Shit. Alright. Yeah, next week sounds great. Sure. Alright. Take care of yourself. Stay outta trouble. (*Laughs.*) Alright. You too, bud. See ya.

(MARK hangs up the phone. Opens it back up again, looks for another number. Focus shifts to next section of stage: a separate memory occuring at the same time. PAUL and AMY lounge on a sofa in AMY's apartment, cuddling. PAUL'S arms are lazily draped around AMY as they watch a movie on a television set.)

AMY

You awake, kiddo?

PAUL

Huh? Yeah. Sorry. I dozed off.

AMY

It's a good movie if you just pay attention.

PAUL

Oh, yeah, I bet. It's just been a long day.

AMY

Paul. It's 10:30 on a Saturday. You didn't work today.

PAUL
That's probably why. Lazy days kill me.

AMY
Maybe we should just go to bed.

PAUL
No. *(Pause.)* Nah, I can stay up and watch this with ya.

AMY
Okay.
  (Pause.)
You don't always have to keep moving to stay awake.
  (PAUL shrugs and rubs AMY'S arms.)
You don't.

PAUL
I haven't learned that yet, Ames.

AMY
Yet. Yeah. I'm gonna get some water. You want anything?

PAUL
Nah. I don't need anything.

> *(AMY leaves the room. PAUL sits up, stretches. AMY walks back into the room with a glass of water and sits down. He takes it for a sip.)*

AMY

Hah. Yeah, you don't need anything.

PAUL

A sip.

AMY

You're something, Paul.

PAUL

Something funny?

AMY

Sometimes.
(PAUL laughs, nudges AMY gently in the side.)
You are. Why I like you. Can't figure you out for anything.

PAUL

The great mystery.

AMY

At least you're self-aware.

PAUL

So what can't you figure out?

AMY

I dunno. Someti– sometimes I —

(PAUL'S phone rings. He gets it out of his pocket.)

PAUL

Sorry, Ames.

(Answering phone.)

Hey, Mark. Nah, not too much, man. You? Cool. Yeah! Yeah, lemme ask Ames if she wants to go, too.

(To AMY.*)*

You want to go get a drink with Mark?

AMY

No.

PAUL

(To AMY.*)*
C'mon. Quick drink.

AMY

No. Paul, we were going to watch this movie.
(Pause.)
Let's talk about this when you get off the phone. Just tell him I'm not in the mood. I mean, you can go if you really want to.

PAUL

(To MARK*)*
Mark? Hey. Looks like she's not gonna come out. Yeah. I'll see you in a couple minutes. Alright. Great. See you there.

(He hangs up the phone, starts getting up.)

AMY

Hold up.

PAUL
What's wrong, buddy?

AMY
You're just leaving?

PAUL
Um. Yeah. You said I could.

AMY
Paul, sit down for a minute.

PAUL
The movie?

AMY
Paul, forget the movie. Look, we've been dating for a year now.

PAUL
Yeah.

(AMY raises her hand to signal PAUL to not say anything.)

AMY
It just feels like things have changed.

PAUL
Well, yeah, A. They have.

AMY
And I don't —

PAUL

But just because things have changed doesn't mean it's bad. We're just getting used to each other in different ways.

AMY

Yeah. Maybe it's that, but —

PAUL

We're fine. Don't worry.

AMY

I dunno, Paul. I just get this feeling sometimes that—

PAUL

Ames, we're fine. Don't worry so much. I just had a long day. And I feel a little drained.

AMY

And you're going out for drinks?

PAUL

It'll wake me up.

AMY

Really.

PAUL

Trust me.

AMY

Paul, I hate to say this, but —

PAUL
Being out will wake me up. Trust me, A.

AMY
Okay.

PAUL
I'll be back later.

AMY
You promise? None of that "uh, I'm just gonna go crash" stuff?

PAUL
I'll be back tonight.

AMY
Alright. When?

PAUL
I dunno – when the bar closes, I guess.

AMY
Don't drink too much.

PAUL
Yes, Mom.

AMY
Paul.

PAUL
Joke.

(PAUL gets up and walks to the door. AMY follows him.)

AMY

Drive safe.
(PAUL nods.)
I love you.

PAUL

(Kissing her on the lips.)
Good.
(He smiles.)
See you later, buddy.

(PAUL heads outside and walks down the hall. AMY returns to the sofa and brings her knees to her chest, cuddling them. She peers out over their tops, eyes glazed and fixed on the television. Lost.)

III.

Scene: in memory. Ten months before first scene. In the dorm, laundry room. MARK *stands by a washer; his clothes rest in a carrying hamper. He uses his card in the swiping terminal – it doesn't work. He continues to press buttons, swiping his card quickly, repeatedly.*

PAUL, *carrying a duffel bag of dirty laundry, walks in as* MARK *does this. He drops his clothes by an empty washer.*

PAUL
Terminal acting up again?

MARK
To say the least. I hate this thing.

PAUL
Lemme try it.   What washer number?

MARK
It's a dryer. Dryer 4.

(PAUL *slowly glides the card through the card reader, presses buttons for dryer 4.*)

PAUL
There ya go, man.

MARK
Hey. Thanks, dude.

PAUL
Sometimes that reader can be tricky.

MARK
Yeah. Whatever happened to quarters?

PAUL
It's easier for the university to steal from you with a card. This thing doesn't print receipts. Y'press the wrong button and your money's gone. Kinda genius.

MARK
Yeah. Never thought about it like that.
(PAUL *begins unloading his laundry into the washer.*)
I never thought I'd see another person down here this late.

PAUL
Haha. Yeah. I learned freshman year that everyone tries to do their laundry on the weekend. So I come down here late on weeknights, do a couple loads.
(PAUL *finishes loading his machine.*)

MARK
Yeah, me too. You can do it all at once, too.

Nothing's taken.

PAUL

(As he swipes his card and starts the washer.)
Kinda genius, eh?
(MARK laughs.)
Well, 26 minutes until this is done. See ya, buddy.

MARK

Yeah. See ya.

> *(PAUL exits. MARK sits on top of a washer, opens a textbook, and begins reading. Pause. PAUL returns.)*

PAUL

Hey. I'm Paul. What's your name?

MARK

Mark.

PAUL

Yeah, I see you around a lot.

MARK

Yeah.

PAUL

Hey, I was just gonna head up to— Oh. Sorry, man. I don't mean to interrupt you studying.

MARK

Nah, I'm just reviewing some stuff.

PAUL

Oh. You wanna come up to my room for a beer while we wait?

MARK

Um. Yeah, sure.
(MARK hops off the washer, carries his textbook with him. They walk to PAUL'S room: a separate memory location. They enter. MARK stands awkwardly at first, surveying the room. It's well cleaned.)

PAUL

Make yourself at home, man.

(MARK sits down on a futon. PAUL tends to a pile of wrinkled button-downs, starts hanging them up.)

MARK

You have a roommate?

PAUL

Nope. He moved out earlier this year to live with a friend. I don't think housing knows I have this to myself.

MARK

Lucky man. Comfortable. Clean, too.

PAUL

Yeah. I try to keep it that way.
(MARK fumbles with his book. Silence.)

Oh, hey, I'm sorry. Let me get you a beer.

MARK

Oh, thanks, Paul.

(PAUL heads to his mini-fridge near MARK.)

PAUL

What kind do you like?

MARK

Do you have any PBR?

PAUL
(Looking at him with disgust.)
Um. No.
(MARK is quiet.)
That's disgusting.

MARK

Um —

PAUL

I don't trust anything that's still proud of an award it won a hundred years ago. And I don't trust the people who drink it.
(MARK shifts in his seat.)
I'm just messin' with ya, man. Lighten up.
(He tosses MARK a bottle of Miller High Life.)

MARK
(Laughing a bit.)
Thanks, man. Hey, um —

(He gestures for a bottle opener.)

PAUL

(Smiles.)
Geez, needy. Hand it 'ere.

(PAUL twists it open for MARK, chuckles as he hands it back. MARK sips it. PAUL gets a bottle for himself.)

PAUL

Ahem. Cheers.

MARK

Oh, yeah. Cheers.

(They tap bottles. PAUL goes to the pile of wrinkled button-downs and begins putting them on hangers.)

PAUL

Feel free to turn on the TV, man.
(He tosses the remote to MARK.)

MARK

Thanks, dude.
(MARK turns on the TV, flips through channels. Pause.)
You gonna iron those?

PAUL

Nah. The wrinkles tend to disappear sometime during the day. And – of course – wrinkled shirts

impress the ladies.
(MARK laughs.)
Makes 'em proud. Actually, two things: One, I don't have an iron. Two, I don't know how to iron a shirt.

MARK

You could always check one out at the front desk.

PAUL

What use is it if I don't know how to use it?

MARK

Haha. You're pitiful.

PAUL

Yeah, I'm kinda proud of the fact that I don't have any clothes that aren't wrinkled.
(PAUL laughs to himself, but catches himself when he notices that MARK is quiet.)
Y'alright? Beer taste funny?

MARK

Nah, dude. It's really good. I might switch.

PAUL

Yeah, it's a good one. "Miller High Life: Champagne of Beers," as it's known.
(Laughs.)
If it says it is, then it must be.

MARK

Yeah. Guess that's better than some old award.

PAUL
(Laughs.)
Of course.
(He hangs up last shirt.)
All done.
(He goes to sit with MARK.)

MARK
You goin' home for fall break?

PAUL
When's that again?

MARK
This weekend.

PAUL
Oh, like two days from now.

MARK
Yeah, if you follow a calendar.

PAUL
That wasn't funny.
(He smiles, gives MARK a playful punch.)
Joke. No, I'm actually staying here for break. I'm from here anyway, so I can really go home whenever. You?

MARK
Nah, I usually fly home, but not now. Gets to be too much.

PAUL

Yeah, it can be expensive.

MARK

That, too.

PAUL

Where you from?

MARK

Florida.

PAUL

And you're coming to school in this landlocked hell when you could be near the beach?

MARK

Hah. It's not as great as it sounds.

PAUL

Bullshit.

MARK

Well, imagine spring break. All these annoying college students invading town.

PAUL

And girls gone wild.

MARK

I see your point.

PAUL

I shouldn't say that. My girlfriend'd kill me. Feminazi.
   (MARK laughs.)
Nah, I'm kidding. She always rolls her eyes when those commercials are on TV. I guess they are kinda dumb. I mean, who wants to see a bunch of titties for an hour?

MARK

Titty montage.

PAUL

I know, right?

MARK

A friend of mine got one of those tapes once.

PAUL

A friend?

MARK

Yes. A friend.

PAUL

Sure?

MARK

Yes. A friend who was not me. Anyway, he said it was too much. He called it "areola overload."

PAUL

I'm fine with that!

MARK

He'd say, like, "Yeah, man, it's boob after boob after boob. Like, they don't stop, man. It's, like, fuckin' areola overload, man."

(They laugh.)

PAUL

Yeah, I'm surprised one of those commercials hasn't come on yet.

MARK

For real, dude.

(MARK takes a final swig, sets it down between his thighs.)

PAUL

That was quick. You done?

MARK

Yeah. Was good.

PAUL

Want another?

MARK

No, thanks.

PAUL

Some other time.
(PAUL wraps his hand around the top of the bottle, pulls it out from MARK's thighs, sets it down beside

the futon. Pause.)
You datin' anyone?

MARK

Nope. Single right now.

PAUL

Yeah. Free to be with whoever you want.

MARK

That's the idea.
(Pause.)
What time is it?

(PAUL leans toward the clock, positioned near MARK, and squints, barely brushing against him.)

PAUL

Three?

MARK

What time did we come up here?

PAUL

Not too long ago. You worried someone might try to get your clothes?

MARK

Oh, no. Just have class in the morning.

PAUL

What time?

MARK

Nine.

PAUL

Shit.

MARK

Yeah, early. But I might pull an all-nighter, do this laundry.

PAUL

An all-nighter for laundry?
(Laughs playfully at MARK, then smiles.)
Do it. I already am.

MARK

Yeah. Yeah, sounds good.

(PAUL pats MARK's knee as he gets up.)

PAUL

We should check on our clothes.

(PAUL shotguns the remaining beer.)

MARK

You could've finished that when you got back.

PAUL

Wouldn't be as cold. C'mon.

(They head back to the laundry room, move their clothes from washer to dryer, dryer to hamper.

> *Finishing before* MARK, PAUL *waits at the doorway.* MARK *finishes.)*

PAUL

'Nother beer?

MARK

Let's do it.

> *(They go to* PAUL's *room.* PAUL *again holds the door open for* MARK. PAUL *gets two beers, opens them, hands one to* MARK.)

PAUL

Cheers.

MARK

Shouldn't we cheer something? To... To what?

PAUL

To areolas?

MARK

To areolas!

> *(Bottles ping. They laugh.)*

IV.

Scene: in memory. Three and a half years ago. On one half of the stage: PAUL's *parents' house. Kitchen with a dinner table, chairs.* ADAM *sits at the table, expecting.* PAUL, *at age 18, enters, heading to the toaster.*

PAUL

Hey.

(ADAM nods a greeting. PAUL twists open the bag of bread, grabs some slices, and adjusts the toaster.)

ADAM

Y'ever been in a fight?

PAUL

Huh?

ADAM

Recently.

PAUL

Whaddaya mean?

ADAM

Have you ever been in a fight.

PAUL

(Turning on the toaster.)
Yeah.

ADAM

Who won?

PAUL

We bo—
(ADAM throws a hard, yet playful, punch into PAUL's chest. Pause.)
Wh—?
(ADAM punches PAUL again. Serious. Hard.)
Man, what the —
(ADAM pushes PAUL hard, begins to brawl. Caught off-guard, PAUL is pinned easily.)

ADAM

Fight back, sissy.
(Without hesitation, PAUL punches him. Then again and harder. They both struggle. There is nothing playful in their fight anymore. ADAM is entirely passionate. If he physically could, he would beat the shit out of PAUL in these moments. PAUL eventually punches ADAM in the gut. ADAM cringes.)
Dude. Aw, fuck, man. Fuck.
(ADAM screams in pain.)
Fucking Christ, man.

PAUL

Adam. Adam, c'mon, get up. Adam. Man, you o—

(ADAM lunges toward PAUL, pinning him down, punching him once in the side.)

ADAM

Never let your guard down, man. Never let your fucking guard down.

(PAUL is defenseless. The toaster finishes. The smell of burnt toast. ADAM punches PAUL one last time, releases him, and stands above his curled body.)

Man, you gotta be careful. I don't want anything to happen to you. Y'never know when something might.

(ADAM stands for a beat, then exits. PAUL struggles to get up. He finds he is well – hurt, but not damaged. He musters up enough energy to stand and throw away the toast. A silence as he holds himself.)

(A shift to a separate memory: MARK's parents' house. Post-funeral. Post-mourning. Dinner one night with MARK and FATHER. MARK, at age 18, enters with beverages: a glass of tap water for himself, a can of beer for his FATHER. FATHER brings out containers of sour cream, a bag of grated cheddar cheese, and ranch salad dressing. All are nearly empty. He brings out turkey leftovers on a fancy serving plate, as well as baked potatoes, small tossed salads, cranberry sauce from a can. He sets down a plate in front of MARK.)

MARK

(Out of habit.)
Thanks.

> *(MARK and his father eat in silence at the dinner table, sitting close to one another. At any moment a word could be said to push the intense silence toward contempt. During the meal, FATHER eats sloppily, scraping hard his silverware against the plate. He begins to sip beer after each bite, with each sip turning slowly into guzzles. He works to scrape the last amounts out of each container onto his baked potato; he smacks and shakes the salad dressing container over his salad. By choice, MARK eats his meal dry, quietly. He glances at his father throughout the scene; FATHER does not respond, even as the glances turn to short stares. MARK stares at his father, holding his fork over his last bite of turkey. He breaks the glance by stabbing the last morsel, shoving it in his mouth, scraping the fork clean with his teeth. He clears his dishware as he chews. FATHER holds his breath, stops chewing, and waits for a response that never arrives.)*

V.

Scene: in memory. Four years ago. Split scene between PAUL's *parents' house and* MARK's *parents' house. Both* PAUL *and* MARK *are at age 17. The scene with* PAUL *occurs in his high school bedroom. The scene with* MARK *happens in a living room. Both scenes should be lit well throughout. The scene playing should never be overpowered by the secondary one. Savor all moments.* PAUL *enters with* RON.

PAUL

So. Whaddaya wanna do?

RON

You always ask that.
*(*RON *kisses* PAUL, *passionately.)*
Aw, you can give more tongue than that.
*(*PAUL *lets out a sighing laugh before deeply kissing* RON.*)*

PAUL

We should turn the TV on, just in case someone hears.

(Shift focus: MARK *sits in the living room of his*

parents' house. JAKE, MARK's younger brother, enters the room and sits on the couch with MARK.)

JAKE

What's on TV?

MARK

I dunno. Aren't you leaving for your date soon anyway?

JAKE

Yeah, as soon as Mom's ready. Why?

MARK

You're wearing that?

JAKE

What's wrong?

MARK

Nothin'.

JAKE

What?

MARK

Really, Jake, it's nothing. You just look like you got dressed with the clothes under your bed. That's all. Susan'll be proud.

JAKE

Fine, I'll change.
 (JAKE heads to his bedroom.)

God, you're acting like Mom.

MARK
(Maternal and mocking.)
Lord's name in vain, deary.

(MARK laughs; JAKE groans and walks to his bedroom. Scene shifts focus to RON and PAUL.)

RON
Jesus. What now?

PAUL
Ron. I like ya, man, I do —

RON
Not this again. Don't pull out your Bible again, and read verses while my dick's still out.

PAUL
Ron, it's n—

RON
(Zipping up his pants.)
Fucking Christ.

PAUL
It's not about the Bible, man.

RON
Then what?

PAUL

Calm down, Ron. I'm only messin' with ya. I like you mad. Kinda hot.

RON
(Looking away from PAUL.)
Such an asshole.

PAUL

Ron. Ron, look at me.
    (Pause.)
Go lock the door.
    (Shift focus: JAKE and MARK.)

JAKE

Better?

MARK

Nope.

JAKE

How can you tell, you aren't even looking at me.

MARK

I don't have to.

JAKE

Okay, Buddha, what now?

MARK

I bet your shirt's wrinkled. And the back right pocket of your jeans is ripped.

JAKE
They're my favorite jeans!

MARK
And the back pocket is ripped.

JAKE
Okay, I'll change. Again. Christ.

MARK
Lord's na—

JAKE
Go to hell.
(JAKE heads out to change. Scene shifts focus: RON and PAUL; RON has moved to kiss PAUL's now-bare stomach.)

PAUL
Shit, that feels so good.

(Without words, RON expresses his love for PAUL; they kiss. Shift focus: JAKE and MARK.)

JAKE
Okay. I'm not changing anymore.

MARK
Your shirt's still wrinkled.

JAKE
I don't have any clothes that aren't wrinkled!

MARK
Well, don't tell Susan that.

JAKE
Fuck off, man!

MARK
(Laughing.)
I'm tryin' to help you, idiot.

JAKE
Susan doesn't give a shit if my collar's messed up. She doesn't care what I look like.

MARK
Did she say this to you?

JAKE
Yeah.

MARK
Jake, she's lying.

JAKE
Susan wouldn't lie to me.

MARK
Welcome to the world, dude. That's what girls do.

JAKE
I'm gonna fight you, jerk.

MARK

You couldn't.

JAKE

Try me.

MARK

Alright. C'mon, little man. Let's fight.

JAKE

You want a piece of this?

MARK

Gimme your best shot, kid.
  (JAKE goes to punch MARK. MARK guards it.)
Wait. Take that shirt off first. Wouldn't want to wrinkle it.

JAKE

Jerk.

(They wrestle. Scene shifts focus: PAUL and RON.)

PAUL

No, keep your shirt on. Should we just jerk each other off?

RON

Do you have a condom?

(Shift focus: MARK and JAKE, with MOM off-stage.)

MOM (O.S.)
Boys! You're gonna break something! Don't make me come up there.

(Scene shifts focus: PAUL and RON.)

RON
What's wrong?

PAUL
We shouldn't do this here. My brother will be—

(Shift focus: MARK and JAKE, with MOM off-stage.)

MOM (O.S.)
I've told you a hundred times. Never mess around in the house like this.

JAKE
Relax, Mom!

MARK
Yeah, Mom. We're not gonna break anything.

(Scene shifts focus: PAUL and RON.)

RON
Relax. I know what I'm doing.

PAUL
But—

                              RON

Shh. It's okay, buddy.

> *(RON looks away as he begins to make love to PAUL. Shift focus: MARK and JAKE, with MOM off-stage.)*

                           MOM (O.S.)

Jake, we've gotta go.

                              JAKE

Okay, Mom.

                              MARK

We'll fight later, kiddo.

> *(Scene shifts focus: PAUL and RON. RON covers PAUL's mouth as he cries, kisses away his tears. Shift focus: MARK and JAKE, with MOM off-stage.)*

                           MOM (O.S.)

Jake, come on. Let's not be late picking Susan up.

                              JAKE

I'm coming, Mom!
  (To MARK, mimicking MOM)
Susan. Don't be late.

                           MOM (O.S.)

I heard that, smart ass. Hey, Mark, I'll be back later tonight; I'm meeting up with Josephine for dinner. Your father's gonna reheat some leftovers for you two.

MARK

Okay, bye, Mom.
   (To JAKE)
See ya, jerk.

(Shift focus: RON and PAUL.)

RON

(Kissing PAUL's cheek)
Shh. You're alright. You're alright.

(Equalize focus. JAKE leaves; MARK sits on the sofa, flipping through television channels. He has a sinking feeling, not knowing why, but does nothing to remedy it. Reasons that it might just be a pang of hunger.

As RON continues to make love to PAUL, ADAM appears outside the bedroom door. Heavy knock. PAUL cries out. Darkness.)

VI.

Back at the bar in the first scene. The repeated present. The bar's set has shifted so that only the outside is seen; all we can see of the dive is through the glass window. Together, MARK *and* PAUL *walk out of the bar. The door slams shut, and the bartender begins closing: dimming lights, locking the door. Standing on the sidewalk under the sterile intensity of the streetlight, the sound of the street envelopes* MARK *and* PAUL; *while they can still be heard, there is more effort in their interaction.*

PAUL

You goin' this way?

MARK

Nah, over there.

PAUL

How you gettin' home?

MARK

Oh, it's not too far. I'll walk.

PAUL
I have my car, man. I could stop by your place on my way to Amy's.

MARK
You're driving?

PAUL
Yeah, I'm fine, man. Just a little buzz.

MARK
Sure?

PAUL
Absolutely. No worries, man.

MARK
Alright. Take it easy. Shit, it's almost three.

PAUL
Yeah. It is.

MARK
Will I see you later?

PAUL
Um, yeah, I hope. Sometime, man. Gimme a call this weekend.

MARK
Cool. Night, dude.

                    PAUL
      (Extending a handshake.)
Peace.

                    MARK
      (Laughs.)
Fuck that, gimme a hug.

                    PAUL
      (Blocking MARK.)
Dude. What?

                    MARK
A. Hug. A hug?

                    PAUL
No.
      (Pause.)
Hah, man. I'm buzzed, but I'm not drunk.

                    MARK
      (Moving in.)
Dude, it's a hug.

                    PAUL
Man, stop.

                    MARK
What, afraid I'm gonna grab yer ass?

                    PAUL
Don't touch me.

MARK

Dude —

PAUL

Don't!

MARK

Alright. I. Won't give you a hug goodb—

PAUL

I'm not like that.

MARK

Neither am I. Peace. Drive safe, bro.

> *(MARK exits, leaving PAUL alone. A long pause. As the sound of the street continues, a slow fade to black.)*

Almost

Thanks for the Scabies, Jerkface!

Button-Down Showgirl

My Parents Talk to Stuffed Animals

acknowledgements.

The author would like to thank the University of
Kentucky and the Kentucky Center for the Arts
for their generous financial support.

Thanks also to Tom Wilkins, Nancy Jones,
Herman Daniel Farrell III, Nelson Fields,
Joan Rue, Bo List, Shayla Lawson,
Carolyn Sesbeau, Mike Giurgevich, Ellen Hagan,
Daniel Cothran, Tim Miller, Vidyuta Rangnekar,
Amy Salloway, Erin Keane, and Trish Clark.

Thanks for the Scabies, Jerkface! received its world premiere on May 19, 2006, at the Firebird Studio in Lexington, Kentucky, and was developed and toured with the generous support of the University of Kentucky and the Kentucky Center for the Arts Governor's School for the Arts Toyota Alumni Performance Fund. It was directed by Tom Wilkins.

In the summer of 2006, the play was featured in the Cincinnati Fringe Festival, Provincetown Fringe Festival, The Berkshire Fringe, KC Fringe, Minnesota Fringe (where it was the top-selling show in its venue, earning Fringe Encore), and the Columbus National Gay and Lesbian Theatre Festival. It was also performed one evening in a commandeered classroom at the Massachusetts Institute of Technology, until the police removed the performer from the premises.

(This play is performed with a set of three identical armless chairs. The actor rearranges these chairs to seamlessly move between locales: dorm rooms, doctor's offices, beds, cars, and other places. The chairs are merely a vehicle for helping to forward the narrative and should never be the sole focus of the performance. Section titles are not spoken.)

pack yer bags.

August 20. 6:55 AM. Today I am moving out of my parents' house and in to college. I'm ready to meet new people, enjoy raucous parties, stay up so late it's morning, and – well, I suppose, somewhere along the way – learn something.

With the help of the army of volunteers, my parents and I move all my stuff into my tiny dorm room in Harvey Hall. My roommate, Darryl, is from western Kentucky. He's an engineering major and in the Army ROTC. He and his parents don't arrive until the following afternoon, but when I see him he's just as his picture.

Wait. Let me explain.

When I received my housing assignment in the mail, I searched his name on the Internet to see what surfaced. A little stalkerish, but I like to know who I'm living with. I found a few pictures of him in school clubs: Beta Club, National Honor Society, Young Republicans. He wore a Polo shirt. Dark hair cut short. Well tanned. And, Jesus, did he have the most piercing blue eyes.

In our tiny dorm room he shakes my hand hello, and I am immediately struck by the intensity of his stare. Soon our parents leave, and we do the standard get-to-know-you routine. We quickly find that we have computers as a common interest. As we're talking about networking and computer software, he shows me his extensive 30 gigabytes of porn.

Our resident advisor, Jacob, introduces himself as Darryl shows off his porn.

(JACOB.) "Wow, that's quite a collection you've got."

(DARRYL.) "Hey, man, if ya want it, I'll burn it for ya."

Jacob politely declines.

The porn quickly becomes Darryl's defining quality. On his birthday, my friend Margaret and I make him a boob cake. Jacob picks up a couple Hustlers to add to the booty. The three of us present the gifts, all of which make him immeasurably ecstatic.

A few days later, I come back to the room to find him standing in his boxers with the porno mags sprawled out on my bed. "Uh, could you take this to the bathroom." Honestly, Darryl's not a bad guy to look at. The Army has treated him well, but I really don't want to be greeted by a half-naked guy standing beside my bed with his fantasies scattered over my comforter. I mean, really, is this how boys bond? Is this how his friends get to know each other?

A friend of his spends the night in our room, and they reminisce about high school. I don't pay much attention to their conversation until I hear them giggling about a game they used to play. A game called Gay Wars.

"Gay Wars? What's that?"

(DARRYL.) "Alright, so we used to play Gay Wars with each other. You'd touch a guy until he freaked, or you chickened out. And whoever got nervous first lost."

So. Heterosexual boys like to act gay with their buddies, and treat it like combat. And if your 'buddy' freaks out before you do, then you win? Win *what*?

"I don't understand. What's the point?"

(DARRYL.) "It's funny."

"How is it funny?"

(DARRYL.) "C'mon, man. It just is."

"Darryl, really, I don't see the humor. 'Hey, let's make fun of gay people'?"

(DARRYL.) "Yeah, man. Man, I'm proud to be homophobic!"

"Oh! Okay!"

(DARRYL.) "What you mean by that? Your friends gay or something?"

"Yeah, Darryl, a lot of my friends are gay."

(DARRYL.) "Oh. Well, I'm not gonna take any of it back."

I finish the conversation with a "whatever, man;" I feel like trying to dig deeper into this, but I'd prefer to not risk coming out while his best friend is here.

Yes, indeed; that's right. I have yet to come out to Darryl. Where I live – and certainly where he's grown up – there's an unspoken don't-ask-don't-tell policy. Coming out for me has not been a problem, but this is the first time in a while where I'm shoved back into the closet. Keeping quiet is especially important in a living situation like this.

I had heard through the grapevine that Darryl had talked to the RAs in the dorm about gay people. Somehow the conversation turned toward the topic of gay roommates. Darryl's response?

(DARRYL.) "I'd move out if my roommate was a queer."

I feel like saying: "Pack your bags; I'm a fag!" But I don't know how well that'd go over. Instead, I play passive and try not to bring it up again.

October arrives a few weeks later, and I start dating Mark, an ex-boyfriend from a year back. We start to spend more time together, but pay careful attention to when Darryl is in the room. On Halloween night, Mark comes over to watch a movie. Darryl has been gone for most of the weekend, so I figure he's gone back to western Kentucky to vote. Halloween has miraculously fallen on a holy Sunday, and Election Day's on Tuesday; maybe he'll skip class on Monday and enjoy a long weekend. Having convinced myself of this, it'll be okay to cuddle with Mark on my bed; I lock the door in case anyone in the hall decides to barge in.

The sun begins to set; Mark and I make out – there's kissing, there's rubbing, shirts come off, more kissing, more rubbing, then — the doorknob rattles. (Oh, shit!) Mark throws me off of him and finds his t-shirt, and we scramble to sit in an acceptable position. As I put my shirt back on I hear the sound of keys being jammed in the door. The door opens, and Darryl walks inside carrying a basket full of clothes.

He flips on the overhead light as I smooth my hair. The fluorescent light fills the room, exposing two boys on a bed – he stops. His blue piercing eyes widen and focus on Mark and me. Something's wrong.

(FATHER.) "Whatcha stoppin' for, son?"

Over Darryl's shoulder is the face of his father, and beyond the two of them stands his mother.

It looks like today's Family Day! How fitting that it's Halloween. In an instant we learn a whole new sense of homophobia: not only scared <u>of</u>, but scared <u>by</u> gay people.

His father stops, too – eyes Mark and me, then nudges Darryl to keep moving.

(FATHER.) "Y'boys havin' fun?"

Darryl's opening and closing drawers, trying to make a racket. His father's eyes are still fixed on me as he inches closer in the room. While staring me down he tugs at his shirt collar. I give him this queer look, thinking 'what are you doing?' My polo shirt's on backwards.

(DARRYL.) "C'mon, Dad."

They exit; the door slams shut, and I hear them marching down the hall.

Mark tells me that he wants to leave. I take him downstairs to check out. On the bottom floor the elevator doors open to Darryl's parents standing at the front desk, their son roaming around the lobby, and Jacob working at the front desk. What a precious picture this makes: the homophobic family and their son's gay pals.

As Mark and I leave, I imagine both of Darryl's parents twisting their necks to watch us. Two sets of eyes bore themselves into our backs, eyes that try to rip. I don't feel bad at all. This is my sense of gay pride: I won't wave a flag in a parade, but I will hold hands with my boyfriend around uncomfortable people.

A half hour later back to the room, Darryl walks inside. He folds towels. He opens and closes his closet doors. He finally speaks to me.

(DARRYL.) "Dan, can we talk about something? Man, you can tell me anything, man, but, man, I have to ask, man. What were you doing – alone – with the door locked – and the lights off – with another guy? Oh. That's cool, man. So. Is it a choice?"

Then we have a conversation about what it's like

being gay: When did I know? How do I know? Do my parents know? How long have I been with Mark? His questions die out, and he hits me with the news I had suspected: his parents want him to move out.

(DARRYL.) "Man, I hate it, but I have to. It's not all about you, man. They don't really like this dorm – but my dad has two rules. One: don't mess with family; and two: don't associate with gay people." That's an enlightened code of conduct.

Days later Darryl's mother calls to say that Daddy had been losing sleep and was nervous about whether or not Darryl would be okay living with "The Homosexual." Maybe he was concerned about me turning Darryl gay. Sure enough, Darryl said that if he did stay, his dad would assume he's gay. For gay people to be stereotypically weak, we sure are assigned a lot of power.

The next weekend Darryl's Army buddies move him across campus. I wake up to him saying goodbye, and then he's gone.

But that evening Mark comes over. Finally, we can be alone. We can kiss whenever we want. And we don't have to worry about anyone barging in. He comes inside, and I'm so excited to see him. I greet him with a kiss, but he's quick to stop me.

(MARK.) "Um, Dan. I'm not too comfortable with this."

"Whaddaya mean? No one's gonna barge in this time."

(MARK.) "No, I mean – this. I don't know if we should – date anymore."

"Oh."

Next thing I know, he walks out the door. The second person to leave my room that day. The second person I'll only see in passing after this moment. This is certainly not the kind of alone time I wanted.

Shit.

smooth-tongued memory.

we run out of there
the flashy lights
the hardcore thumping
pumping out rhythms
bodies slam together
as each strobe light flash
exposes another fleeting photograph.

i wrap my shirt around you close
bite your ear
kiss your temple.

we run out of there,
stumbling through streets
no care, no tact.
nothing stopping us.
the cops bust up the party

for underage drinking
but we run
run so far
because they can't catch us now.
you drive us to your house
not-yet-21: one drink in your system
you speed me away from chaos.

back to your house
we bathe,
standing in the shower
we take turns soaping
embracing
kisses mixed with
the strangely sweet taste of soap.
we rinse mouths
dash through hallways
over chipped floorboards
dodging splinters
and jump through darkness.

you wrestle me to the mattress on the floor
for half my size you have twice my strength
you pin me, face up
my head pushed up

so the pillow cradles my crown
your arms push mine down
and promise to me:
'you can't use these tonight'

two minutes and i gasp
five and i jump
thirteen. my body goes numb.
you collapse on top
fingernails scratch out a pattern on each other's
arms, thighs, back.

in the darkness
we rip at each other
until we've nothing left.

you mite die.

OH. MY. GOD. I have never itched this much in my life. I just woke up to find myself furiously scratching at my thighs. For the past few days I've sat in class and tried to pay attention as I rip at my stomach and forearms. And it's so bizarre – I don't have a rash; it's normal-looking skin that never ceases to itch. The itching isn't bad in the day, as long as I don't think about it. But it is absolutely unbearable at night.

Let's examine my actions of the past week.

I was out of laundry detergent, so I had to use a different brand. The last time I switched brands I broke out in hives. After Mark and I broke up, I met a guy named Drew. I spent the night at his house, and his dog kept jumping on me. I think it was scratching itself. Oh God, what if I have fleas? To make it worse, I'm allergic to dogs.

Not able to stand it for much longer, I ask Jacob if he could take me to buy medicine. We drive to Wal-Mart, and I buy two tubes of hydrocortisone cream and an anti-histamine.

(JACOB.) "So, what do you think it is? Wait – you said you spent the night with him? Did you – y'know? You totally did! You screwed Drew! Oh, I bet you have something weird, like scabies."

"Shut up; no, I don't."

We walk down the aisle to leave and go to the checkout lane. One of Jacob's friends happens to be working. Jacob introduces us with a very presentational voice so that the adjacent lanes hear:

(JACOB.) "Have you met Dan? Dan has scabies."

"Damnit, Jacob. Will you stop telling all of Wal-Mart that I have scabies? I don't go around announcing the time you douched your anus.

I mean, 'Oops!'"

We drive back to the dorms in silence.

The medicine doesn't help much. Realizing that self-diagnosis is not the way to health, I decide to head to the health clinic on campus. As soon as I walk in, a country-accented doctor who constantly mispronounces my name confirms my suspicion about it being laundry detergent. Case closed. I'm given a "'scription," as he calls it; maybe the itching will cease.

I take the medicine, but the itching becomes more prominent. What the hell is going on with my body? Another itch week passes before Jacob says,

(JACOB.) "Dan, I'm not joking anymore. What if you do have scabies?"

I head to the Internet to find symptoms.

"Intense itching, especially at night and over most of the body." Check.

"Pimple-like irritations, especially the webbing between the fingers – " Check.

"The skin folds on the wrist, elbow, and/or knee – " Check.

" – the groin – " Body, what did you get yourself into?

I soon find that scabies is a mite that burrows in your skin, lays eggs, and defecates on your body. The eggs hatch, and the process begins again. Wait – so microscopic critters are making babies and taking shits all over my body? Oh, I'm gonna vomit.

The next day I make an appointment at the campus doctor's office. And the same doctor as before walks in the room.

(DOCTOR.) "Mr. Bernita, what's the problem?"

"It's Bernitt. Y'know – it's cold (brrr), so I'll knit a sweater."

(DOCTOR.) "Ah, Barnett. We needa teach them

secretaries to write."

"I don't care – I still itch all over. At night, during the day – I itch all the time. It's not my laundry detergent – I'm certain. What the hell's wrong with me?"

(DOCTOR.) "Well, Mr. Barnett. I don't think itching's yer problem – seems ta be yer attitude an' tone, son. I din't go to school fer –"

"Sir. I itch all over."

(DOCTOR.) "S'better! Alaska few kestions. Have you used anyone else's laundry detergent?"

"Didn't we already go through this?"

(DOCTOR.) "Imma axe the kestions, son."

"No, sir."

(DOCTOR.) "Slept in any weird places recently? Forests? Shantytowns? Pay-by-the-hour motels?"

"Uh –" What's my doctor insinuating? "I spent the night in a friend's bed."

(DOCTOR.) "Nope, not it."

"Oh, right! Because friends can't possibly give friends diseases!"

(DOCTOR.) "Son, show me where ya itch."

I point out all of the tiny bumps. He grunts and fetches glasses which enlarge his eyes to the size of golf balls.

(DOCTOR.) "Mhmm. Y'ever heard've scabies? Mhm! Say y'itch at night? Mo'rat night than th'day? Yup, prolly. Stop y'groanin'; life's not over, son. Imma wrote you a 'scription fer a cream. You gotta keep it on yer body for 'least eight hours. Itta kill 'em suckers good. Now, you know where ta take this? That's right. Cash it up at the farmacy. Y'might wanna stay away from some friends' beds from now'n. 'Kay, son?"

Yeah, I think I learned that. And I'm so glad that

he's getting a good laugh out of my situation. Well, maybe it is kinda funny. I call my mom at work to inform her of the diagnosis.

(MOM.) "I'm sorry, buddy."

"Yeah, gross, eh?"

(MOM.) "No, I mean, I'm sorry as in I didn't hear you – the phone cut out. You have what?"

"Scabies."

(MOM.) "Oh, baby, how the hell did that happen? Y'know, people die from that!"

"Mom, no, they don't."

She starts telling me the story of Old Yeller.

"Jesus, Mom, I said scabies, not rabies."

Mind you I'm having this conversation with my mother while walking back to my dorm as people are heading to and from class.

(MOM.) "Baby, isn't that one of *those* diseases?"

"Uh, no. It's a dermatological infection. Usually spread through roommates or family members."

(MOM.) "Are you sure? I'm looking online and it comes up under sexually transm– "

"Mom, I have to go now."

I hang up as she offers a piece of motherly advice:

(MOM.) "Well, don't go whoring yourself out, buddy!"

That evening, with my friend Margaret's help (of boob cake fame), we cover my body with the scabies cream. As she rubs it into my skin, I notice on the packaging that one of the possible side effects is death, but I could care less. Death is on the agenda tonight: whether it's the scabies or me, this itching will stop. Sure enough, it did.

It wasn't until a few days later that the Harvey Hall scabies epidemic took place. Margaret, who slept in my bed one night, ended up itching. The gods of karma took their revenge on Jacob and infested his body with mites. And a guy who lived two floors below my room woke up to the bug. Margaret tells me one night as we apply cream to her body:

(MARGARET.) "Y'know, that Drew guy seemed alright, but, really, if I see him I'm gonna fight him."

Months pass and one morning I walk down the main campus road towards class. And suddenly in my view is Drew, talking on his cell phone and strutting towards me. We pass each other; he nods a hello, and I force a greeting. I want to go up to him, and say: "Excuse me. Hey, um, I know we haven't talked, or anythig, in a while, but I got, uh – scabies. And just I thought, if you hadn't already checked it out, that, uh – you might want to go do that."

However, tact is of no use to me; he is a fair distance away when I see myself turn towards him, take in a large breath, and ululate to the public: "THANKS FOR THE SCABIES, JERKFACE!"

teach to.

screaming and shouting
I kicked out of the womb.
eight pounds four ounces,
held up by my scrawny legs
and smacked
until I learned to stop my noise.

I became quiet
the reserved little kid
who did as was told,
as expected.
years later I found myself
outside of the parental incubator
inside a brand-new world

I've broken the strings
that once guided me on the way.

that told me what to feel.
finding my scrawny legs
scuffed on the edges
I search for a Geppetto
to fix my joints
to restring me
so I only fit what you want me to be.

teach to eat
teach to talk
teach to walk
to move
dance

teach me to smile pretty
open vacant eyes.

this is not a tv show.

I'll admit it: I'm a sadistic fan of reality TV shows. I love seeing bits and pieces of people's lives taken out of context and woven together to form these terrible misrepresentations. In fact, I love this so much that when I hear that there's a casting call downtown TODAY – for a certain MTV show, I squeal as I run to audition. I find my place in line, and fill out a questionnaire with tricky questions. "Are you in a relationship?" Not anymore. "Are you employed?" Sometimes? "What are you afraid of?" Monsters. And getting scabies... again.

Feeling content with my curt answers, I turn in my form and receive my audition number: 247. By this point there's an enormous line behind me. I'm now one kid in a crowd of hundreds vying to be one of the seven strangers picked to live in a house and have their lives taped! YES! My chances are – slim.

I spend time peoplewatching from my seat, and then my audition group is ready to go. Since there is such a high number of auditionees, groups of ten will sit in a circle with a casting director and each group member will grasp for attention by playing whatever stereotype trump card they can. Among others, there's the smiley black guy, the intensely happy girl whose friends don't realize that she's not always happy, the sweet and sassy Southern girl who loves Michael Jackson, and the short Asian kid with bouffant hair whose family owns massage parlors.

The casting director asks us: "What is the biggest misconception people have about you?" We go around in the circle, each trying to trump the previous answer. The guy next to me says that most people think he's gay, but he's really not. Aha! I'll trump that one! "Well, I'm gay!" Yes, indeed: I have established myself as The Homosexual in order to appear on national television. As soon as I let down my royal rainbow flush, all attention is on me.

The casting director asks me what it's like to be gay in Kentucky, and I make a miffed comment about how I can't kiss guys in public without the fear of being attacked. People start to nod, but the bouffant haired Asian kid has a tidbit to add: "Oh, get over it. I do it all the time." With that quip, he trumps me. Before I have time to respond, the casting director closes the audition. Boo.

A few days pass and I go back to my dorm room one afternoon to find a message – not from MTV, but from the bouffant-haired Asian kid via a college networking website. Apparently his friends think we should date. Intrigued by his frankness, I exchange messages with him for a few days, then phone numbers, and one night I invite him over to the dorms. We spend the evening swapping concert stories and listening to M. Ward, Stina Nordenstam, and Prince.

The next weekend, he calls.

(BOYFRIEND.) "Hey, it's me."

Oh, my God, we're at the hey-it's-me stage.

(BOYFRIEND.) "I'm kinda stuck at my parents' house. My roommate is throwing a party at our apartment tonight, and there's no way for me to make sure nothing gets burned down."

"Well, that sucks. What if I picked you up?"

Using his directions, I navigate my way to his house in my 16-miles-per-gallon minivan. Halfway there I stop to refuel. As money pours into my gas tank, I literally say to myself: 'Oh, Dan. You're spending money you don't have to drive halfway across the state for a kid you barely know.' Yep.

At his house he meets me outside, cautiously gets in the minivan, and chuckles as we pull out of the driveway.

(BOYFRIEND.) "You didn't tell me you'd be rescuing me with a spaceship, Soccer Mom."

The spaceship zooms back to town and stops at his front door. We sit there in silence for a moment. What's an appropriate gesture for this? A handshake?

(BOYFRIEND.) "Well, Dan, if you want to come over in a bit, you can. Give me some time to clean up."

He closes the car door. I pull to the end of the street, out of view. YES!

I grab Margaret, of boob cake and scabies cream fame, and we head to the party. She goes in search of alcohol; I for bouffant hair. Half-stumbling, he emerges from out of a bedroom to greet me. He clutches my arm, then runs to fetch a drink with me in tow.

In the minutes Margaret spent standing in the kitchen, she has already taken a few shots. She begins a warpath: finding people to kiss. A few minutes later she stumbles back in to announce her results.

(MARGARET.) "I KISSED FIVE BOYS AND ONE GIRL!"

Now she's vehement about seeing boys make out.

With each other. In fact, she wants them all to do it in the kitchen. And she's pulled a couple of boys in the room with us.

(MARGARET.) "MAKE OOOOUUUT!"

The two guys glance at each other; I glance at my partner in this pairing.

(MARGARET.) "DOOOO IT! NOOOOOW!"

They decide to strike a deal: they'll make out if we do. And I think: YES! Yes, absolutely, I'd love to! I look over to this guy – and he has a slightly, um, disgusted look on his face.

They proceed to make out, and suddenly I feel a pair of lips on my own. A tongue dips into my mouth occasionally. It tastes like vodka and cigarettes, but –

(MARGARET, *thrashing like a rockstar on an air guitar.*) "YESSSSS! OH, THAT'S SO HOTT! HOTT WITH TWO MOTHERFUCKING T'S! YES-YES YES-YES HO-O-OTT!"

– but I kiss him back. It's new, different. Not fresh, but I like it. Margaret stumbles off, and the two guys disappear – leaving us alone. Later we stumble into his bedroom. In a way I feel a bit tacky – I just arrived at this party and now I'm in the host's bedroom. Oh, first impressions! In his room, he sits on my lap, facing me. In between kisses he says:

(BOYFRIEND.) "I'm sorry I made a face when they told us to make out. I thought you didn't like me."

"Oh, come on! Would I really drive across the state to pick you up if I didn't?"

(BOYFRIEND *shrugs his shoulders, nods.*) "Touché."

As we kiss again, there's a loud thump against his bedroom window.

(MARGARET.) "OH MY GOD! THEY'RE MAKING OUT AGAIN! AUGH! THIS ROCKS THE UNIVERSE!"

With that a group of faces turns to peer inside. He

runs to close the blinds.

(MARGARET *singing*.) "WE'RE LEAVING, DANNY BOY! YOUR PIPE, YOUR PIPE IS CALLING! GET IT GOOD!"

December 11th: the starting point of our relationship. Who'd've thought that out of auditioning for a reality TV show I'd find a boyfriend?

Our relationship rapidly progresses over the following months. He makes me dinner every few nights so I don't have to eat campus food, teaching me how to fry tofu and roll sushi. Valentine's Day comes and we exchange cards, his with the lyrics of a silly popular love song printed inside. It isn't long before we start saying 'I love you' and sharing a bed like a married couple, our bodies spooning. Later, he starts a new job and lists me as his emergency contact. We even start looking at health care plans. Yet as quickly as all of this goes, none of it seems too soon. Like it's all just right.

In the summer, I'm planning to go to Provincetown, Massachusetts, to be in a theatre festival, so for April Fools' Day, we decide to tell everyone that we'll be getting married. Much to our disbelief, everyone is supportive.

(MARGARET *growls*.)

Everyone except for Margaret.

(MARGARET.) "Dan, what the fuck are you thinking?"

"Margaret, it's a joke. April Fools!"

(MARGARET.) "Well, you're a fool for dating him!"

"What are you talking about? He's a good guy."

(MARGARET.) "My ass! What about the fact that he can't accept a compliment without belittling you? What about the fact that you had to drag him to see a play you directed? What about the night he said you were only dating him for sex? Or that he drinks too much? Dan, I'm telling you this cuz I know it. You may have some good times, but you're not being honest with yourself. You're like his little marionette, and you don't even know he's pulling your strings. I hate seeing you like this, man."

"Margaret, you don't understand him like I do. I mean, yeah, he has done all that – I'm not innocent either. But it's in the past now. You can't always hold it with you. He means well. He does."

A few months later I'm performing in a festival an hour away from town. His birthday happens while I'm there, but I send packages to his house, including a brand-new Scrabble board, and I call him at midnight to croon happy birthday over a staticky cell phone connection. He thanks me for them. During our conversation, I tell him my show dates.

(BOYFRIEND.) "I know."

"And even if you don't see my show, I'd like to see you. You can spend the night here instead of driving back."

(BOYFRIEND.) "Um, I don't know."

His apathy stings. And I'm beginning to think

Margaret's right. Funny how our friends see through the things we live. Throughout the two weeks of the festival, each strained conversation ends different: with 'I love you,' or tension, or 'come back soon.'

My birthday falls on the weekend after the festival. I usually don't turn my birthday into a big celebration, but I've never had one while in a relationship. At the stroke of midnight, my boyfriend calls from work to say that his car won't start. When I pick him up, he's sitting out front, flustered. He hops inside; we drive and stop at his apartment; he steps out, closes the door, and walks inside: no goodbye, no i-love-you, no happy birthday.

Okay, he's distracted. His car broke down, and it'll cost a couple hundred dollars to fix. A few minutes after I return to my apartment, he calls, still complaining, but pauses to say: "oh, by the way, happy birthday." As soon as I say thanks, he continues grumbling.

The next afternoon I pick him up in the spaceship. With him sitting by my side, I've never felt so alien around the guy to whom I say, "I love you." I drop him off at work. Still nothing more than a by-the-way. That evening I enjoy the company of my family at dinner and of my friends afterward. And my favorite present came from Margaret, prefaced with: "You can use this whenever your boyfriend's not enough." A dildo.

Midnight arrives, and I pick him up; at my apartment, he says he's hungry. All I have is half of a box of pierogies.

(BOYFRIEND.) "So, Dan, what'd you do tonight?"

"I had dinner with my family, then some friends came over. How many pierogies do you want?"

(BOYFRIEND.) "Whatever the serving size is. You okay, boo?"

How can I tell him how much it hurts that the one person I wanted to spend my birthday with has done nothing more than wish it to me with nonchalance? Right now, I want to hit him. I may be a pacifist, but I so want to pass a fist right into him.

The dildo sits in its packaging on the table. 'Whenever your boyfriend is not enough.' Too bad molded plastic can't make me feel any less unrequited.

As I think this, I realize how whiny I am. Dear Dan: how far into emo-land are you going to go? How can you compare your neglected birthday with his finances? You are being unfair. Listen, kiddo, you got yourself in all this. No one said this was easy. It's part of the territory. Suck it up and deal; or take your brand-new dildo, and go fuck yourself. You met at an audition for a reality TV show, forchrissakes. Is this real world enough for you?

Answer his question: 'you okay, boo?' Don't be so MTV; say something PBS.

"I'm fine."

Okay. So those aren't the most profound of words, but baby steps are worth something. I'm sure of these two words until he stands up from his stool to come hug me. He whispers in the most soothing voice: "I'm sorry I forgot."

I break. All I can think is: I don't want to deal with this – not now. Can't I run away from this, from him? At least until I learn to see with a better sense of perspective. Can't I just –

The timer dings my answer: No. Sometimes when you think you need to be consoled, it's because you hurt someone first. Stop being pathetic, and start being sympathetic. Take your ladle, and dish <u>that</u> out.

"Your pierogies are done."

foreign sheets.

in between hits and highs
he and I lay on the comforter
the navy sheets rumpled, used
not his doing.

I enjoy the friendly warmth
of a body next to mine
open-chest, face up.
we do the same.

as I drift off
he curls next to me
clutches my shoulder
and forces a position
I only want to share with you.

as I lie between naps
lips and mouth caked with morning gunk
haven't-brushed-my-teeth-or-hair-in-days
he presses his lips on mine,
occasionally wiping away
the slime from my mouth, his mouth.
my tongue.

never wanted to tell you
that this happened.
never wanted you to notice
my tight kisses the next night.
a third face eluding us
in our bed.

never wanted to admit
that his lips felt good on mine
even though I meant to resist.
even though I jerked away
from his mouth.
at first.

or admit that I lied
in this unmade bed that I made.

I used to think that
pushed breath and a quick lay
would make me happy.

now all I want
in the morning
is a warm embrace,
a comfortable feeling in foreign sheets,
a face that brings joy.

instead I confront myself
with the fact that though
two bodies lie together in bed,
it doesn't mean there's harmony.

renewed.

Mosquitoes ravage my skin as I eat Chunky Monkey in front of the Ben & Jerry's in Provincetown. I may start itching, but at least it will be nothing like scabies. Itching is the least of my worries, because I'm in Cape Cod for two weeks – away from my family, my boyfriend, and everyone I know.

Since I know no one here, I took my search for a familiar face to the Internet. On MySpace, I sent out a few messages. One responded: Trent, five years my senior. He seems friendly – offering to show me around town, introduce me to people. In the message, he included his phone number and told me not to feel awkward about calling.

I slap a mosquito and give Trent a call. He doesn't answer, but moments later, he calls back.

(TRENT.) "Hey, Dan! It's Trent. I'm walking on Commercial Street right now. Where are you? Whoa, I'm just a couple blocks away. I'll be there in a coupla minutes."

Soon we meet on the street. Jesus. He's like a work of art: deliciously olive skin, eyebrows like acrylic paint over his beckoning brown eyes. His teeth like near-perfect pearls a jeweler uses to show off. Lips open to offer comfort, to guide this newcomer. His stubbled face is like infinite ellipses I find myself vying to complete.

Wait, Dan, what are you thinking?

"Nice to meet you, Trent." We shake hands and converse: our sentences and responses quietly walking one another through a song. But our duet ends offbeat: I am not yet 21 and cannot go to the bar he's invited me to. "Hey, I'll give you a call tomorrow. We'll get lunch."

Trent and I spend every day together. We go to the pool one afternoon, and he buys me lunch. When he finds out that I didn't pack a pair of shorts, he offers me a pair to borrow for the time I'm there, as well as a bike I could borrow whenever I needed it. And with each conversation and adventure, I find myself falling for this guy. We tell each other about our lives and pasts. He's had scabies, too!

But even when he says that he cheated on his last boyfriend and doesn't believe in monogamy, I still long for him. I want this to never end, the joy of seeing him, his sheer kindness and generosity.

In these brief encounters, I nearly forget about my boyfriend. Here is a glimpse of the kind of man I've longed after and only hold in my dreams. The polar opposite of my boyfriend. Now, yes: Dan, try not to be naïve; everything can be perfect upon first glance, and it will all die down ones the realities of a relationship surface. Look at the relationship you're in now. But it doesn't have to be this way. Why should I settle for someone who doesn't fit? But I can't have Trent.

One evening in the guesthouse, my boyfriend calls. I notice our halted conversation.

(BOYFRIEND.) "So, Dan. What have you been doing lately?"

"Well, I've been hanging out with this guy named Trent. We rode bikes around town yesterday, and we went to the pool on Thursday. I think we're going to—"

(BOYFRIEND.) "Dan, please don't talk about Provincetown."

"Buddy, I'm here in town and this is what I've been doing. What else am I supposed to talk about? Trent and I are just hanging out."

(BOYFRIEND.) "Okay. I have to get my car fixed; it's acting up again."

"If I can't talk about Provincetown, could you please not talk about your car?"

Our conversation shifts into an attack on my character. All of a sudden I'm rude, inconsiderate, a bitch, and – evidently – I'm oppressive. What, how, when, why? Where is this coming from? And from the one who says he loves me.

The next afternoon I meet up with Trent and tell him what the boyfriend said.

(TRENT.) "So, why are you dating him?"

With that question I search for answers and excuses. I stutter out something vague, but I cannot find an honest answer. I cannot answer an obvious question. Questions of perspective flood my head.

That night Trent arrives to see me perform. Following the show, Trent comes up to me and says: (*as* TRENT) "I really enjoyed your poetry." A simple comment, but of more worth than he'll ever know. Compliments my boyfriend never says.

On the last night, Trent and I hang out at his apartment, laughing, talking, drinking wine. While I'm there, my boyfriend calls, but I don't answer. I put my phone back in my pocket, and Trent brings out his photographs of the winters in Provincetown. The wine runs through us, and he heads to the restroom.

I lie down on his bed, relaxing. He returns and shuts the door. He puts on music then lies down next to me. All of my desires brim to the top. I am filled with want.

I poke him in his side. Evidently, he's ticklish. My fingertips tickle his clothed stomach more. He tickles me in defense, and then grabs my hands to stop me.

(TRENT.) "Your hands are so soft," he says, feeling my palms, my fingertips. Through touch we compare scars, hands, our rough spots. "Wait – Dan, we shouldn't do this. You have a boyfriend. If you were single, I'd be ripping your clothes off. But I don't want us to ruin something good. I don't want us to regret anything."

He is right. He is so right. It's wrong of me, but here is a guy – he has completely renewed my sense of happiness, redefined what I need in a relationship. I want nothing more in this moment than to share thanks through an embrace, feel the solace of a kiss. I want to share the intimacy I have craved and have spent time trying to force in a relationship with my boyfriend. Here he is – lying next to me, but completely off limits. My hand returns to my side.

(TRENT.) "Well, I didn't mean for you to stop."

I hesitate no longer. I return to caressing, feeling, trying to make him as happy as he has made me. He sits up. I brush my hands on his back, smooth his wrinkled t-shirt, outline his spine with my fingertips.

He turns his head to look at me. Then it's sudden when he throws himself on top. Our lips locking. This is it – sweet, even with the faint taste of alcohol and cigarettes. His hands rest under my back, holding onto me. I remove his hat; kiss him softly on the lips. I play with his hair as his tongue sneaks behind my teeth, feeling my scars like Braille.

We are lovers searching for all the right moves, retelling the stories of past encounters. Telling only the good parts and longing to write an ending better than before.

And as quickly as our kiss begins, it ends. He collapses on top. This brief encounter filled the longing – finally, yes. I'm holding what I have longed for for so long. Remember this – this is what you need. We kiss again, as if to say I am still alive and loveable, then we leave the guesthouse, each going in separate directions, agreeing to meet the next morning before I leave. On the street we kiss again, and part.

That night I can hardly sleep – for thinking about him, and the fact that I now have to head back to my boyfriend, my conscience as my chaperone.

The next morning I meet Trent at a coffee shop by the dock. On a bench we exchange glances, words, jokes – nothing seems enough to make up an ending. My final minutes tick away. I don't want to leave this place. I don't want to leave his side. The boat begins loading. We embrace, my body trying to soak up as much of the feeling as possible. Our clothed torsos touch for the last time; our lips say farewell. I arrived in town feeling starved and hungry; I leave with a new sense of life – surviving off of the memories. The horn blares; Provincetown and Trent fade into the mist.

Back in Kentucky, I drive over to my boyfriend's apartment: holding fast to my actions, to my decisions, rehearsing what I will say. I must be honest with him, but how? How does this come up in conversation? I walk upstairs to his bedroom. On his bed is the Scrabble board I bought him for his birthday. He sits there, a smile on his face.

(BOYFRIEND.) "I set this up for us. I thought you might want to play a game."

I join him on the bed, and he begins drawing letters from the bag. How can he quickly go from being the jerk who insulted me while I was on vacation to being a caring and thoughtful boyfriend? How can such a simple gesture completely change a situation? And why is it that the simple things always bring us to our knees?

I start to draw letters from the bag, but get Q and R and W and X and L and O and T. Qrwxlot. Qrwxlotta nothing. If only the Scrabble gods had the humor to offer: F-U-C-K-M-E. And a blank.

(BOYFRIEND.) "You first, Dan-o."

"I got nothing."

My mind floods with phrases like "I can't deal with this." I felt sure of everything, but now –

"Boo, I can't do this."

(BOYFRIEND.) "There's no need to be so dramatic, Dan. The theatre festival's over."

He smiles at his joke. If he only knew.

(BOYFRIEND.) "You can draw again if you want."

"No. No, buddy. We need to talk. Y'know, we said this while I was in Provincetown and even before I left. Maybe we should break up. You're right. We aren't making each other happy; maybe we should see other people to find what best fits us. I found while I was in Provincetown and while I was hanging out with Trent –"

(BOYFRIEND.) "Dan, I don't mean to sound childish, but was there anything going on between you two?"

"Yes; yes, we kissed the last night I was there."

Nothing more.

He is silent. He sits across from me, pushing the letters around on his Scrabble rack. Silent. He shoves the board aside, leaves the room to smoke, then comes back and sits in a chair. I move off of the bed to try to talk to him, my hand resting on his back. He tells me not to touch him, not to rub his back, but he doesn't want me to stop. We sit at opposite ends of the room, his back to me, the tension looming. Later he comes to the bed, sits next to me, and kisses me. Kisses me hard.

(BOYFRIEND.) "What does he have that I don't?"

I search for responses to articulate all the differences, all our shortcomings to each other – all this as familiar lips enclose mine, sealing the answers inside. Even though I'm holding steady to my decision, I don't want to leave the familiarity of my boyfriend, no matter how right it would be. But I can't stand up to my own convictions because I'm too scared of being alone.

(*Pause.*)

At long last, this reveals itself.

He says he doesn't want to be alone either. But how do we move past this?

once eluded.

I closed the phone
saying goodbye for the last time.
You know how much I hate the word.

For the first time in my life
I sat mute –
at a standstill in my swivel chair –
unsure of what to say.

Wanting the first word out of my mouth
to sum us, to justify it,
to give credence to the end.

The next night I let it out:
with swig after swig
and hit after hit
as I sat between levels on the stairs

the railing my crutch
in either direction.
my hands weighing vodka and pot:
the two substances that punctuated us.

At the start
with your tongue coated with liquor
to the night I stumbled back to the dorm
finding you in between my sheets:
you told me I smelled like hash.
as you rolled to the other side of the pillow.

somehow I made my way outside
slid down the vinyl siding
cool from the August night
from the shade of the oaks.

People scamper in and out
yelling shouting screaming
laughing talking drinking
but I'm alone with your insults.

churning through my belly,
spinning through my veins,
escaping in breaths from my chest.

I puked.

I vomited so hard,
spewing out of my mouth
with each thought:

"you're a bitch." My chest heaves.
"you are so inconsiderate."
                My head like held breath
                'til I pop.
"rude."   Chunks.
"asshole."   Throat burns.
"you only love yourself."
                A rush so hard there's blood.

I lean back: gasping, choking for air,
eyes half-closed.

He comes outside:
this figure I've never seen before
he pats my back:

'y'alright?'
"I feel like ten kinds of dammit."
'let's get you outta here, kid.'

He fastens me in his car,
and we slowly careen through the summer streets
I lean the seat back and stare at the ceiling;
the streetlights sweep my face.
I breathe in the summer air
wipe away the acid from my lips.

I offer a joke to color the silence:
"I'm sure the grass is dead."
He chuckles, rubs my crown

Soon we pull to my back porch.
We leave his car
       he's my crutch for a moment
       until I realize I can stand upright.

Turning the keys in the lock
he pulls me away
and kisses my lips

And I think:
       'No. Not this again.
       This is not what I want.
       This is not what I need.'

"get rested up, pal. you're still alive."
A kiss as if to say I'm still alive and loveable.

He smiles, turns, and leaves
as I close the door.

Looking through the peephole
I see him turn on his car again.
I wait until the driveway clears
to turn off the porch light.

awake.

Tonight I will head to my bed alone. A thought that used to scare me. Of course there's a time when I'm disappointed and heartbroken – loving from afar. There are times when I want nothing more than to fit together with someone else like a puzzle piece. For now, I clutch my pillows and wrap myself in a blanket, soaking in the warmth of my bed and the coming dreams. And whisper to myself: "you'll be alright, kid."

I say goodnight. Goodnight to the one who drove me to my door, his hand lingering on my cheek as he bid me adieu. Farewell to Trent, as we stood at the loading dock, as we used to stand each night by his front door. I kiss the old boyfriend to sleep after I had crawled between the sheets, wrapping my arms around his torso. I say a nice goodbye to all of the mites that burrowed in my flesh, and the boy who gave them to me. I shout an "OH MY GOD!" to Margaret, my fellow felon. And I remember the nights at the beginning of the year when Darryl and I would say goodnight to each other from our separate sides of the room. All these moments bridged a gap between us.

I leave like we leave lovers: far too soon to get the real loving done. But a content smile turns euphoric on my face. And, for now, I'm home.

I am home.

(Slow fade to black as DAN *prepares his bed and lies down to sleep. Curtain.)*

Almost

Thanks for the Scabies, Jerkface!

Button-Down Showgirl

My Parents Talk to Stuffed Animals

acknowledgements.

The author would like to thank the Crown and Anchor Bar 'N Grille. And Margaret Cho, who was there (!) and – surprisingly – didn't find her way into the monologue.

Button-Down Showgirl was first performed at the Kentucky Governor's School for the Arts in Lexington, Kentucky, on July 3, 2007.

It later found its way into a collection of performance pieces entitled *Thanks for the Scabies, Jerkface! (And Other Stories)*, which premiered at the Indianapolis International Fringe Theatre Festival in Indianapolis, Indiana, on August 24, 2007.

Once upon a time. (July 10, 2006.) In a land far, far away. (Provincetown, Massachusetts.) Exists a time of day when the women dress as women, and so do the men. (At dusk on Mondays.) On this particular Monday, like all summer Mondays at the tip of Cape Cod, hundreds of vacationers and townies gather to see Showgirls, a weekly cabaret at the Crown and Anchor Bar 'N Grille. With advertising copy boasting of "innocent spectators caught in a sinister web of indecent costumes and halfway decent acts," how can I not want to attend? Or, rather, noticing the $500 cash prize, how can I not want to participate? For a second time.

In the summer of 2005, I traveled to Provincetown to perform a one-man show in a theatre festival. Finding my audiences after the first weekend to be less than desirable (attendance = zero), I signed up for the event to advertise. Halfway through that night of Showgirls, I hopped onstage, performed a piece of poetry, and – even though the host mocked me during my shtick – received a pretty positive audience reaction. The Judgment wrapped up the evening with me in the top four. Narrowed down to the top two, I thought I was bound to win against a less-than-fabulous drag queen.

Suddenly, the host interrupts.

(RYAN.) "Excuse me, Dan. Didn't you say you were doing a show in town? Sorry, no professional acts can win the prize. Off the stage, honey; lots of drag queens here to win."

Professional act? I'm flattered, but flattery can't help a college student pay for a room at a guesthouse – even here in Provincetown. Marching offstage, I vowed a rhyme:

'For 2006, I'll have some new tricks:'

A group of men transform into new personalities backstage at the Crown and Anchor. New personalities who adjust their wigs, stuff their bras, and lip-sync to whatever show tune plays on the portable stereo. Dressed in a button-down and khakis, I stand out against their glitter and pancake makeup. A butch shorthaired woman walks up to me and asks if she can help me. "I'd like to sign up for Showgirls," I announce. She purses her lips and gives a quick nod. "Lemme know what you're doing and your name." Poetry. Jacob MacAdams.

My body sits introspective with hands clutching journals, while the queens bustle around me, sharing sassy one-liners and lipstick. Next, the woman announces the line-up. Out of seventeen is "Number 8: Jacob MacAdams." Right towards the middle, I strategize, right when the audience gets warmed up. Performers before me walk backstage and comment about the audience: "Man, it's a great audience out there. Everyone's really warming 'em up."

I tear away from the gripping entertainment of gender bender stardom, and stand in the hallway by the stage.

(RYAN.) "Miss Twanzwaited, everybody! Give her a round of applause! Next up is a fabulous drag queen from here in town. You all know the routine by now. Please welcome: Sharon Needles!"

The audience seems warm and encouraging. This is great; I've got this in the bag! The money's mine. I think all this until I hear the sound of beer splashing and plastic cups crashing against the stage. A ditzy drag queen croons off-key to something Sondheim, punctuating each of her key changes with "Now, that's not so nice" or "Oh, silly geese, just stop!"

Note to self: don't mess up.

(RYAN.) "Sharon Needles, better luck next week. Next up is – (*laughs*) We have a special treat for you all tonight. There's a poet in the line-up."

I cringe: so soon! I have to do something edgy. And quick!

(RYAN.) "Yes, a poet. As long as he keeps it under three minutes, I say 'sure!' And if he brings the mood down, feel free to throw more beer up here. Please welcome to the Showgirls stage, Jacob MacAdams."

"Hello, my name is Jacob MacAdams, and I go to Oberlin College," I announce to the audience of mostly older hairy gay men. Beginning one poem I realize there's no way to pause my three-minute shot for five hundred bucks. No way to add or subtract from my performance after this. What to do. Something edgy. If I don't do something, the beer will come soon.

I finish a fast-paced slam poem and gently segue into another short poem, this one much more sensual than the last. My hands find their way to my button-down. My fingers begin unbuttoning as curious grunts and the shifting of seats hit my eardrums. Shirt unbuttoned, then off, now pulled taut by my hands like a towel in a locker room, my voice continues with the next stanza as my eyes spot the shirt falling to the beer-covered stage, the fabric seeping amber as more words spill out of my mouth.

My ears catch a curious and intrigued yelp from an audience member: "Is he a stripper poet?" Arms lower to my belt as my mother's voice enters my head: "Keep it in your pants while you're in Provincetown, Dan."

Fingers unbuckle the belt as the climax of the poem nears. Belt whips from its loops, fly unzips at the climax, black boxer-briefs expose themselves to the silence. My throat huffs out the final lines. My chest heaves with the rhythm of the previous words; I stare blank at the neon alcohol advertisements on the back wall.

"Thank you."

I snap to the reality of having just strip-teased for a group of gay men and gather my wet clothing. Ryan announces my name to an uproar of applause. As I scurry backstage, buttoning my shirt, I wonder if it was edgy enough, if what I ended up doing is still considered risqué.

Nine acts and fifty minutes later, Ryan asks all of the nonprofessional acts to return to the stage for the final judging, a judging based solely on audience applause. Out of the seventeen, four appear – I am the only non-drag contestant. Cheers and applause for the drag queens, but what seems like thunder rumbles for the poet. The group narrows down to two: I am one of them. Again, same judgment.

(RYAN.) "Okay, Jacob has clearly won. But I think Miss Terectomy should have to arm wrestle Jacob for twenty dollars. Whaddya say? Someone get a bar table up here."

A stagehand grabs a table and chairs as I think to myself: Um, I don't remember armwrestling being part of the rules. Then Ryan pipes up:

(RYAN.) "Who thinks they should kiss?"

This, too, was not in the deal.

(RYAN.) "Come on, Jacob, kiss the drag queen."

The audience cheers for the idea. I find myself weighing moral issues – should I kiss a stranger for money? – until I realize that removing one's shirt and exposing one's undergarments in a performance setting in exchange for a known monetary amount has a colloquial term for an act far worse than kissing.

Stripping myself away from overthinking a situation, I offer a quick peck on the lips.

(RYAN.) "Oh, kiss her with tongue!"

The moral dilemma royal flush starts arranging itself again in my hand until the stripping trump card halts any further action. Go ahead, 'Jacob,' I tell myself. At least you listened to your mother about keeping it in your pants; she never did mention anything about keeping that zipper closed. One brownie point in your favor as the audience cheers you on.

(RYAN.) "I thought he was straight! Jesus! Alright, guys, calm down, calm down. Count them off for the arm wrestle match."

The audience howls, and I suddenly find myself in an arm wrestling match against a drag queen. We compete, and I suddenly find myself losing an arm wrestling match against a drag queen.

The audience groans.

Emasculated, I walk offstage to the dressing room. Ryan pats my back to congratulate me.

(RYAN.) "Let's get you your money."

He begins counting the cash by the mirror where earlier plenty of men fashioned themselves into something they're not for a chance at the same prize.

Ten. Twenty. Wow, so, I just won cash. *Thirty.* Lots of cash: humiliation = mass payout. *Forty. Sixty. Eighty.* Did I really just do that? I wonder if I could've won by just doing poetry. *One hundred. One twenty.* It's all just for entertainment though. *One forty. One sixty.* But I wonder what those guys out there think. Do they think I'm some kind of floozy? *One eighty. Two hundred.* Wait – if anything, that was Jacob's doing. I was a character tonight. *Two ten. Two twenty. Two thirty. Two forty.* No, Dan, that's a lie. You can't separate yourself from that. You are Jacob. *Two fifty. Two seventy. Two ninety. Three ten.* At least I made more money for performing for three minutes than I will with my show in the theatre festival. So, it's been profitable. *Three twenty.* Yay, capitalism. *Three forty. Three sixty.* And I'm leaving town soon. No one will really remember me. Let alone know my real name. *Three eighty. Four hundred.* It's not like I got completely naked. *Four fifty. Four seventy. Four seventy-five. Four eighty.* And it's not like I did anything to compromise my integrity.

Well –

The next afternoon I share the news with my mother, leaving out certain details. She says she's proud.

(MOM.) "Your father will be so excited to hear this."

Out on the streets of Provincetown, right when I think the excitement has passed and I've returned from the bizarre limelight to being just another tourist, an older gentleman eyes me outside the library. He extends a hand and asks: "Hey. Aren't you Jacob?"

Almost

Thanks for the Scabies, Jerkface!

Button-Down Showgirl

My Parents Talk to Stuffed Animals

acknowledgements.

The author would like to thank Ed McClanahan and the faculty, staff, and fellows at the Gaines Center for the Humanities.

My Parents Talk to Stuffed Animals was first performed in a classroom under the tutelage of Ed McClanahan at the Gaines Center for the Humanities at the University of Kentucky in Lexington, Kentucky, on April 12, 2007. (Performance art has to get its start somewhere, even classrooms. Especially if commandeered.)

It later found its way into a collection of performance pieces entitled *Thanks for the Scabies, Jerkface! (And Other Stories)*, which premiered at the Indianapolis International Fringe Theatre Festival in Indianapolis, Indiana, on August 24, 2007.

My parents talk to stuffed animals.

I have thought of countless fancy ways to begin this story, but – my parents talk to stuffed animals.

At the age of three my mother would read me bedtime stories: *The Berenstain Bears*; *Alexander and the Terrible, Horrible, No Good, Very Bad Day*; and some pink hardcover book that, while with flawless illustrations and a to-die-for typeface, had no literary merit whatsoever. Trust me, I knew: I was three. Once when one of these stories failed to put me to sleep, I demanded for my mother to tell me a story.

(MOM.) "What story do you want me to tell?" She asked.

(KID DAN.) "Tell me a story about Puffalump," I said.

Puffalump was a badass stuffed yellow monkey with white yarn hair and a Hawaiian shirt. Not only that, but he was my badass stuffed yellow monkey with white yarn hair and a Hawaiian shirt. In fact, my mother knew Puffalump was so badass that her tale featured him stealing blueberries from the grocery.

I started bawling.

(KID DAN.) "Puffalump, why'd you steal the blueberries?!"

My mother would often have to reassure me that it's just a story, and there's no reason to get worked up over such a thing. Besides, I was supposed to be falling asleep. But how can a kid fall asleep when he finds out that his stuffed animal, his best bud, his son has become a thief? Noticing my peril and paternal disappointment, she quickly wiped my tears and moved the plot to its resolution: Puffalump apologizes to the grocer and pays for the blueberries with his allowance.

Bedtime stories would occasionally consist of tales about Puffalump, with my mother weaving together anecdotes and alternate character voices when I asked for stories about some of my other stuffed children. After a few nights, she grew tired of my orchestrations, resigning with "Not tonight, Daniel." While the stories disappeared the character voices still remained: Puffalump telling me to go to bed, Puffalump singing songs in his deep baritone voice, Puffalump hollering for someone to catch him as he flew down the staircase. It became a family ritual, and eventually they would sit in an apron as the family ate dinner, and coming out to play as we finished dessert.

While I hate to admit that this routine continued well into my high school years, it kept a humorous mood in the house, filling a house of introverts with multiple personalities. I'd bring the stuffed animal downstairs for dinner. My mother would play with a stuffed dog as she drank a glass of wine. After wrangling it out of her hands, my father made it act crass.

(MOM.) "Dwayne, I mean, Nous-Nous, it's not polite to fart at the table," my mother would say.

(DAD.) "But I'm just a dog!" My father would

defend, making the animal throw its hands in the air in innocence. "That's what dogs do!"

As my sister left the table dismissing us as "weird," the stuffed animal channeled through my father to shout, (*as* DAD) "Hey, Meagan! Look what I can do!" He'd make a sonata of farting noises as the toy Shar Pei danced around on the table. My father often laughed himself to tears this way.

Nous-Nous arrived after I had surgery, as a get-well gift addressed to me. My mother liked the dog immediately, occasionally taking him out of my room while I rested to bring him into the kitchen to cook with her. Nous-Nous's temperament emerged as one typical of Shar Peis: intelligent and snobbish. After getting well, I walked downstairs one afternoon to find my mother with Nous-Nous standing by the window.

(MOM.) "Nous-Nous saw a squirrel running around outside," my mother informed me.

(NOUS-NOUS.) "Res, rye raw ruh ruirrel running r'around ron ruh rass," Nous-Nous said.

"What?" I asked.

(MOM.) "He saw it running around on the grass," my mother explained.

Apparently Shar Peis speak in a language where all words start with R. To tell the dog his name is Nous-Nous is like asking a man who lisps to identify his speech impediment.

(MOM.) "We're having chicken pesto for dinner."

(NOUS-NOUS.) "Ramma, rorrect ree riff rhyme rong, rut rye rearned rat resto ras rine ruts rinit."

(MOM.) "Yes, Nous-Nous, pesto does have pine nuts in it. You're such a smart dog! Let's go make some. Doesn't that sound like fun?"

***

In college, voicemails and phone conversations with my parents would include some kind of mention of Nous-Nous. The dog would join them at dinner in restaurants, hiding in my mother's purse until it was safe to take a peek and sit on the table. During two summers Nous-Nous vacationed with my parents to different parts of the country. Not only did the puppy see the Kentucky, Ohio, and Mississippi rivers in one car trip to Arkansas, but this knowledge allowed him to skip from kindergarten to third grade. The second summer he flew to Hawaii, leaving the continental United States before I had the opportunity. While my parents took pictures of the dog sitting on an airplane seat, napping after a snack of trail mix, and exploring the rocks on the beach of the Big Island, I packed up my dorm room by myself.

College continued: I became busier, and the stories about Nous-Nous grew more complex. Sometimes I would just not answer the phone because I didn't want to have to try comprehending what the hell was going on in their little Dogworld. One night I answer:

(DAD.) "Hey buddy, I'm sitting here with Mom and Nous-Nous."

Nous-Nous, via my mother, in the background:

(*as* NOUS-NOUS) "Rello, Raddy!"

(DAD.) "Listen, uh, your dog has been acting up."

"And what did <u>my</u> dog do?"

(MOM.) "Nous-Nous, tell your daddy what you did."

She changes voices: "Raddy, rell, rhere ruz riss rully rat rool, rand – " The dog begins to blubber. My mother consoles it, switching between blubbering in caninespeak and consoling in English: "Nous-Nous, if you can't – ROO-ROO-ROO-ROO-ROO – if you can't tell your daddy what you – ROOOOO ROO-ROO-ROO – Nous-Nous, I guess I'll just have to tell him what you did."

(DAD.) "Nous-Nous got into a fight at school. A bully was picking on him. Yep, this pitbull started harassing him on the playground."

"Uh-huh," I say.

My mother and father continue back and forth for

several minutes as I walk down the street to rehearsal for a play. I hear something about a pitbull hassling Nous-Nous about traveling to Hawaii. Apparently the pitbull and his bully friends wanted proof of Nous-Nous's travels, the stuffed dog said he'd bring them to school tomorrow, but the pitbull demanded to see the photos now. Pitbull bites Nous-Nous, Nous-Nous bites back, and the teacher watching over recess sees Nous-Nous attacking the pitbull.

(NOUS-NOUS.) "Rand row rhyme rurended!" Nous-Nous howls.

(DAD.) "Can you believe that! The justice system at his school. Nous-Nous was just defending himself, and now he's suspended."

"Yep. That justice system in – Dogland. Hey, I'm at rehearsal now, can I call you all back tomorrow?"

(DAD.) "Sure, Dan. Give us a call then. Maybe by then we'll have everything sorted out."

"Sure, Dad. Sure thing."

At the time I was directing a campus production of *The Vagina Monologues*, a play usually sponsored and supported by organizations dedicated to ending violence against women. Nous-Nous found out about this aspect of the play.

My mother, when I call several nights later: (*as* MOM) "You would be so impressed with Nous-Nous. Well, remember how that pitbull attacked him? Well, Nous-Nous started a campaign on his campus to end violence against dogs. Guess what he's calling it? Bark Loud! He has such a fun sense of humor."

My father barks in the background.

(MOM.) "They even have these little wristbands that they wear. Well, they're not really wristbands; they're more like pawbands. He's very resourceful. You'll have to see them when you come home for Easter. He's growing up so fast. Well, we better let you go. See you Sunday."

I hang up the phone and think: Gee, if the dog had thumbs, he'd sign the papers to start a nonprofit.

All this from a puppy who used to just fart at the dinner table. Who thought he'd end up being so precocious?

For Easter my family usually has dinner together. My sister and I go to our parents' house and enjoy a home-cooked meal. As the years have passed since we were both in high school, it's now one of the few times we all get to see each other. In fact, whenever we're all gathered around the dinner table, there are moments when it seems like nothing has changed: my mother still plays with the dog as she drinks a glass of wine, my father still makes it act crass, my sister still thinks they're "weird."

As we leave, they hug us goodbye, saying, "We love you." I pull out of their driveway and drive back to my apartment, thinking all along about the damned stuffed dog. I arrive home, latch the door shut, and sit alone in my apartment.

Brushing my teeth I imagine them in their home, sitting together, the house silent now that my sister and I have moved out. Sometime during their day, they pulled their puppy out of his bed – much like they'd wake us up – slid him down the staircase railing and cheered him as he landed on his feet. At dinner, they'll talk about their day, asking Nous-Nous how his day was. As they watch TV, the dog sits perched on the sofa, joining them in their evening. Later they, too, will latch shut the front door and head to bed, tucking him in his little bed. They'll kiss each other goodnight and fall asleep.

Sitting alone in my apartment I can't help but to feel empty as I imagine this, and think that my sister's and my absence may've in any way caused this.

I sigh away all the times I could've spent more evenings with them, the times I wasn't able to come home for dinner, the times I said I'd call but didn't. I sigh away responsibility and reassure myself that at least they're happy – after thirty years of marriage – at least they can laugh together as they make up these stories.

Besides, I tell myself, it's just a story. There's no reason to get worked up over it.

 Dan Bernitt's solo performances (*Moments of Disconnect*; *Thanks for the Scabies, Jerkface!*; *Phi Alpha Gamma*) have been featured in venues internationally: from Minneapolis and Cape Cod to New York and Dublin. He is a recipient of grants and fellowships from the Kentucky Center for the Arts, the University of Kentucky, the Kentucky Arts Council, the Robert Chesley Foundation, and the Helene Wurlitzer Foundation of New Mexico. His books, *Dose: Plays & Monologues* and *Phi Alpha Gamma*, have been named finalists for the Lambda Literary Award.

He is a summa cum laude graduate of the University of Kentucky's arts administration program. He has also served as creative writing assistant faculty for the Kentucky Governor's School for the Arts, a program of which he is a graduate. A Kentucky native now living in New York City, he is an MFA playwriting candidate at The New School for Drama.

www.danbernitt.com

www.ingramcontent.com/pod-product-compliance
Lightning Source LLC
Chambersburg PA
CBHW031258110426
42743CB00040B/735